# The Skiing Handbook: Your Thrilling Beginner's Guide to the Slopes!

Published By: Rylie Lane

Copyright © 2024 by Rylie Lane

All rights reserved.

No portion of this book may be reproduced in any form without written permission from the publisher or author, except as permitted by U.S. copyright law.

**Table of Contents**

WHAT IS SKIING?............................................................4
SKI GEAR ......................................................................10
YOUR FIRST TIME SKIING .......................................16
DEALING WITH NERVES AND BEING SCARED 24
WHAT TO EXPECT AT THE MOUNTAIN ............27
MOUNTAIN SAFETY ..................................................44
SKI SCHOOL - WHAT TO EXPECT ........................52
AFTER SKIING - TAKE CARE OF YOUR GEAR, WAYS TO RELAX ........................................................60
EMBRACE YOUR SKIING ADVENTURE ..............69

## What is Skiing?

Imagine waking up to a world covered in sparkling white snow, with everything from trees to mountains wearing a thick winter blanket. You step outside, feeling the cool air on your cheeks, and you see a big mountain slope stretching out in front of you. This is where skiing begins! Skiing is a special way to travel over snow using long, flat boards called skis. People all around the world love skiing for the fun, speed, and beauty it brings, as well as the way it lets them enjoy the outdoors—even in the coldest months.

In this chapter, we'll learn about the basics of skiing, a little about its history, and why it's such a fantastic sport. Whether you're a beginner or have been on skis before, you're about to dive into a world of snowy fun!

## Types Of Skiing

In the simplest terms, skiing is a way of moving across snow by gliding on two narrow boards called skis, one attached to each foot. People use special boots to attach their feet to these skis, and they usually hold poles in their hands for balance. Skiers use their bodies to control their speed and direction, and with practice, they can turn, slow down, or go faster by changing the way they position their skis on the snow.

There are different styles of skiing that cater to everyone from thrill-seekers to those who prefer a peaceful glide through the snow-covered woods. Here's a quick guide to some popular types:

1. **Alpine or Downhill Skiing**
   This is probably what you picture when you think of skiing. In downhill skiing, you take a lift up to the top of the mountain and then ski down trails that vary in difficulty. Downhill skiing is the perfect place for beginners to start, and resorts usually have trails to suit every skill level.

2. **Cross-Country Skiing**
   Unlike downhill skiing, cross-country skiing doesn't require mountains or steep slopes. Instead, it involves skiing across flatter, snow-covered ground. This type of skiing is popular in places where the landscape is snowy but not mountainous. It's great for building stamina, and people often ski through beautiful forests and snowy fields.
3. **Freestyle Skiing**
   This style is all about creativity and fun! Freestyle skiing includes jumps, spins, and tricks, usually in specially designed parks with ramps and rails. It's like skiing's version of a skate park, and it's incredibly exciting to try or even just to watch.
4. **Backcountry or Off-Piste Skiing**
   For the adventurous souls, backcountry skiing is about heading off the marked trails and into untouched snow. It's a little more challenging and requires experience and avalanche training, but it offers a way to connect with nature away from the busy slopes.

While there are many styles of skiing, we'll focus on downhill skiing in this guide, as it's the easiest and most common way for beginners to get started.

## History Of Skiing

Did you know that skiing is one of the oldest forms of transportation? People have been skiing for thousands of years! The first skiers weren't doing it for fun—they used skis to travel across snowy land for hunting, gathering food, and exploring. Archaeologists have found ancient carvings and cave paintings that show people skiing in northern parts of Europe and Asia over 5,000 years ago!

In the 1800s, skiing had become a popular sport in the Nordic region of the world. People started racing on skis and new developments of ski technology enabled riders to move faster and with more control. By the 1930s skiing was brought over to north America and the first ski resorts and lifts were built. From there skiing spread to all over the world!

## Why Do People Love Skiing?

There are so many reasons why people love skiing! Here are just a few:

1. **It's Fun and Exciting**
   Skiing gives you a feeling of freedom and excitement. There's nothing quite like the thrill of skiing down a mountain, the wind rushing past as you glide over the snow. Each slope and turn feels like a new mini-adventure, and for many people, it's the most exciting way to spend a winter day.

2. **Beautiful Scenery**
   Skiing lets you experience winter in some of the most beautiful places on Earth. Picture snow-covered mountains, towering pine trees, and wide-open skies. Many resorts are set in breathtaking spots where the views alone make the trip worth it.

3. **It's a Great Workout**
   Skiing keeps you active in the winter, and it's a great workout for your legs, core, and even arms. Balancing and controlling your speed require strength and coordination, which means skiing is great for staying healthy and active, and it can make you feel strong and energized.

4. **Time with Family and Friends**
   Skiing is a fantastic activity to share with others. You can ski alongside your family, race your friends, or even take ski lessons together. Many people make skiing a part of their family's winter traditions and look forward to it every year.

5. **Learning New Skills**
   Skiing challenges you to learn and improve. From making your first turns to conquering a challenging slope, each skill you master builds your confidence

and makes skiing more fun. You'll always have new goals to reach!

Today, skiing is enjoyed all over the world, and has become a popular winter sport that millions of people love. Skiing is an amazing sport that lets you explore snowy landscapes, learn new skills, and have tons of fun. Whether you're skiing down a mountain, trying your first cross-country trail, or watching ski competitions on TV, there's always something exciting happening in the world of skiing. So, are you ready to join the adventure?

## Ski Gear

Before you can hit the slopes, you'll need to gather the right gear. The essentials range from the skis that help you glide to the helmet that keeps you safe, and the cozy jacket that keeps you warm in the winter chill. Here's a breakdown of the essentials you'll want for your first ski adventure:

## Essentials

1. **Skis**

   It all starts here! Skis are what let you glide over the snow. They come in different shapes, lengths, and materials, but for beginners, it's easiest to rent a pair suited to your height and weight. At most ski resorts, the rental shop staff can help fit you with a set of skis that'll work well as you learn.

2. **Boots**

   Skiing requires special boots that snap right into the skis. They're a bit more rigid than regular boots to give you the control you need on the slopes. Like skis, ski boots come in various styles, but don't worry too much about picking the perfect pair on your own—ski rental staff are trained to help you get a snug, comfortable fit.

3. **Poles**

   Some people think poles are just for experienced skiers, but they're actually helpful for beginners too. They'll help you balance and move on flat areas. Some ski schools suggest beginners skip poles on the very first lesson so you can focus on learning to balance without the extra coordination, but once you're comfortable, poles become a handy tool.

4. **Helmet and Goggles**

   Safety first! A helmet is essential for all skiers to protect your head in case of falls or unexpected bumps. Goggles help you see clearly and shield your eyes from the bright sun reflecting off the snow, which can be blinding.

## Layering Up For the Slopes

It's no secret that mountains get cold! The trick to staying warm while skiing is to layer your clothing properly. Here's a simple, three-layer approach to stay cozy on the slopes:

1.  **Base Layer**

    Base layer is the first layer that is used. It consists of thermals or what some people call long underwear. A base layer is a long sleeve top, tights, and socks and is typically made of warm material. The thermals should be fitted and shouldn't be baggy when you put them on so they don't get bunched up under the other layers.

2.  **Mid Layer**

    The mid layer goes over the base layer. It typically consists of a warm puffy jacket, flease jacket, or hoodie. You can also include a mid layer pant if its extra cold outside, but a mid layer pant is often too warm for most people. When in doubt include the layer as you can always take it off if it gets too hot.

3. **Outer Layer**

    The outer layer is your waterproof shield against the elements. Your ski jacket and ski pants keep you dry from snow and act as a windbreaker, helping you stay comfortable all day. Don't forget gloves to keep your hands warm and dry.

Depending on the temperature outside and weather helps you determine how many layers need to be worn, when in doubt wear the layer, if it gets to hot there is always the option to take it off.

### Accessories

Now that you know of the basic of dressing for skiing, there are additional accessories that you can have, both functional and for fun!

- **Neck Gator/ Balaclava**
  A Neck Gator and Balaclava will help keep your neck warm. They also help protect your face if its windy outside
- **Helmet Cover**
  A helmet cover is a fun way to express yourself on the mountain

### Clothing Tips

1. Don't Bunch up your socks! When putting on your socks either put your thermals over your socks or your socks over your thermals. Make sure there is no bunching of fabric on your shins so when you put your boots on there are no pressure points.
2. Keep your toenails short! Ski Boots are meant to be fitted and that means there isn't much more room in there other than your foot. If your toe nails a bit long there is potential to jamb them while you

ski. Before you go skiing double check your toenails to make sure they aren't too long
3. Tuck in your shirts into your ski pants. When you put on your ski pants make sure your tops are tucked in, this keeps the warm air in while you ski and makes sure you don't get snow down your pants if you fall!
4. If you have long hair, put your hair in a low pony or braids to help it from getting tangles. Helmets are essential for skiing, but they can cause our hair to get tangled throughout the day.

## Your First Time Skiing

Alright, you're geared up and dressed in layers—now what? The first time on skis can feel a bit intimidating, but remember, everyone starts somewhere!

## Skiing Basics

When learning to ski there are 3 main skills you should focus on first: gliding, turning, stopping. There are multiple ways to accomplish the above, but if its your first time skiing you should start small and build up your difficulty level as you improve.

### Getting Used to Your Ski Gear

Before you start skiing, you have to make sure you are comfortable in your boots clipped into your skis. Once you are clipped in move around a little to get a feel for the skis, lean forwards and backwards, left and right to get an understanding of how the skis move when you shift your weight.

### Getting into a Skier's Stance

Before you start moving try getting into a skier's stance while clipped into your skis

1. Stand with your feet shoulder width apart

2. Bend your knees and lean forward into your boots
3. Keep your arms slightly in front of your body
4. Keep your eyes on where you want to go don't look down at your skis

**Your First Glide**

Before you attempt skiing down a hill, you first want to get a feel for gliding with skis. The flat ground is helpful so you will naturally come to a stop and don't have to stop yourself

1. Get into your skiers' stance
2. Ask an adult to give you a push to start the glide, or use your poles to help
3. Make sure you keep your skier's stance throughout the whole glide, keeping your skis parallel. When your skis are parallel this is often called frech fries!

**Tip!** it is common to lean backwards as the skis move we want to avoid this by keeping the weight evenly distributed and knees bending into the ski boot

### How to slow down and stop

The easiest way to slow down and stop on skis is to do a called pizza or snowplow. This is when the tips of your skis are close together while the back of the skis are further apart creating a triangle shape. Try on flat ground first and work your way up to a gentle slope.

1. Get into your skier's stance
2. Ask an adult to give you a push , or use your poles
3. First start off with french fry skis
4. As you are gliding widen your skis into the pizza shape to slow down and eventually stop
5. Tip: the wider your pizza the slower you will go, once on a hill to start again narrow your pizza to start moving again

**Tip!** Don't cross your skis or you will lose control

## How to Turn

By the time you are learning to turn you should have had practice gliding on gentle slopes. To turn you want to use your legs to direct the skis and keep your upper body neutral

1. While gliding, put more weight in your left leg to turn right
2. then put more weight in your right leg to turn left
3. When you are shifting weight you can control your speed with adjusting the size of your pizza

## Beginner Drills

### Walking up hills

To walk up hills get your skis perpendicular to the slope so you don't start sliding, then take little side steps to make your way up the mountain. Another way is to get your skis in a backwards pizza facing directly up the hill and take steps from there.

### Pizza and French Fries

Going downhill alternate between pizza and frech fries to adjust your speed throughout the run

### Linking Turns Together

Turn left for two seconds, then turn right for two seconds linking multiple turns together

### Hokey Stops

While gliding make a sudden turn to one direction skidding to a stop, try to spray the snow as high as you can

### Falling and Getting Back Up

Falling is a natural part of learning to ski, and it's nothing to be afraid of. Even the best skiers fall sometimes! The key is knowing how to fall safely and how to stand back up again. Here's what to keep in mind:

- **How to Fall Safely:**
  If you feel like you're going to fall, try to relax and fall to the side instead of forward. Bend your knees and try not to stick your hands out too far to avoid hurting your wrists. Falling on your side helps you slide gently into the snow.

- **How to Stand Back Up:**
  Getting back up on skis can be tricky, but with a little practice, you'll master it! Here's how:

  1. **Position Your Skis:** After you've fallen, roll over onto your side and make sure your skis are across the hill, not pointing up or down it. This keeps you from sliding away as you try to stand up.
  2. **Push Up with Your Hands or Poles:** Place one hand (or both if needed) on the ground or use

your ski poles for balance. Push yourself up into a kneeling position then standing position keeping your skis perpendicular to the slope.

3. **Start Skiing Again:** Once you're standing, take a breath, make sure everything is comfortable, and start skiing again!

# Dealing With Nerves and Being Scared

It's completely normal to feel nervous or even a little scared the first time you try skiing. Being in a new place, trying something you've never done before, or seeing steep slopes can make anyone a bit anxious. But guess what? Those feelings are part of every new adventure! Here's how you can handle your nerves and turn them into excitement:

- **Start Small:** You don't have to ski down a big hill right away. Begin on the small, gentle slopes to get comfortable. As you gain confidence, you can try bigger runs.
- **Breathe:** When you feel nervous, take deep breaths. Breathing deeply helps you relax and focus.
- **Positive Thoughts:** Instead of thinking about what might go wrong, try to focus on what could go right! Tell yourself, "I've got this!" or "I'm getting better every time!"
- **Go at Your Own Pace:** Don't feel rushed to ski like everyone else. It's okay to take your time. Everyone learns at their own speed, and that's what makes skiing fun.
- **Focus on Fun:** Remember why you're here—to have fun! Laughing with friends, sliding on the snow, and enjoying the beautiful outdoors is what skiing is all about.

## Finding Confidence When Trying New Things

As you start to feel more comfortable on skis, you'll be ready to try new challenges, like skiing on steeper hills or learning a new technique. Here's how you can find the confidence to take on these exciting new things:

- **Celebrate Small Wins:** Did you make it down the hill without falling? Awesome! Did you master the pizza? Great! Each small win brings you closer to bigger goals. Celebrate them!
- **Ask for Help:** If you're unsure about something, ask a friend, family member, or your instructor for advice. Learning from others can give you the confidence to try something new.
- **Take Breaks:** Sometimes, nerves build up when you're tired. Taking a break for hot chocolate or sitting by the fire can

give you the energy and confidence to try again later.
- **Visualize Success:** Before you try something new, close your eyes and imagine yourself doing it successfully. Picture yourself turning smoothly, skiing down a new hill, or getting on the lift with confidence. This can help you feel ready when it's time to try.

# What to Expect at the Mountain

## How to read the Map and Run Rating System

**1. The Ski Map**

When you arrive at the ski resort, you'll probably notice a giant map posted near the lodge or at the base of the main ski lifts. This map is like a big guide that shows all the trails, ski lifts, and important locations on the mountain. Here's what you'll usually find on a ski map:

- **Trails and Runs:** Each trail (or run) is marked by a line that winds down the mountain. Trails have different colors and shapes, which we'll explain in the next section.
- **Ski Lifts:** These are marked by straight or zigzagging red lines , showing where each lift begins and ends. Lifts take you from the bottom of the mountain to different starting points so you can ski down.
- **Important Spots:** Ski maps often show places like the ski lodge (where you can warm up and grab a snack), first aid stations, and sometimes even where the best views are!

Before you head up the mountain, take a moment to look at the map and find trails that match your skill level. It's a good habit to keep a copy of the map in your pocket or on your phone too, so you can check it anytime while skiing.

## 2. Run Rating System

Every ski trail has a rating to show how easy or hard it is. Resorts use a color and shape system to rate trails. Here's how to understand each level:

**Green Circle (●): Beginner**

- **What It Means:** Green circle trails are the easiest on the mountain. These trails are usually wide and gently sloped, which means they aren't too steep and are perfect for beginners.
- **Who Should Ski Here:** If it's your first time skiing or if you're still learning, look for green circle trails. These runs will give you plenty of space to practice your turns and stopping without going too fast.

**Blue Square (■): Intermediate**

- **What It Means:** Blue square trails are a bit steeper and narrower than green

trails, which makes them a bit more challenging but also more exciting.
- **Who Should Ski Here:** Once you feel comfortable on green trails, you can try a blue square run. It's a great way to build your skills and confidence on slightly tougher slopes.

**Black Diamond (♦): Advanced**

- **What It Means:** Black diamond trails are for advanced skiers. These runs are steep and sometimes bumpy or narrow. They may have moguls (big bumps on the trail), tree paths, or other obstacles.
- **Who Should Ski Here:** Black diamond trails are best for experienced skiers who are confident in their control and speed. If you're ready for more of a challenge, black diamonds will definitely give you one!

**Double Black Diamond (♦♦): Expert**

- **What It Means:** Double black diamonds are the most difficult trails on the mountain. These runs are often very

steep, with difficult terrain like cliffs, moguls, or deep powder (fresh, fluffy snow).
- **Who Should Ski Here:** Only expert skiers should try double black diamond trails. These runs require strong skills, quick reflexes, and lots of experience.

### 3. Special Trail Markings

Some ski resorts also use other symbols to give you extra information about certain trails:
- **Orange Oval (Freestyle Terrain):** This symbol marks areas that are specially designed for tricks, jumps, and obstacles. Freestyle terrain is fun, but you should only enter if you know how to handle jumps and bumps safely.
- **Slow Zones:** Certain parts of the mountain, especially around beginner areas or near the base lodge, are marked as "slow zones." These areas are meant for slower skiing to keep everyone safe, especially kids and beginners.

## The Magic Carpet

Imagine gliding gently up a snowy slope without having to hike or struggle—just stand still, and the ground itself will carry you! That's the magic of the "Magic Carpet." It might sound like something from a fairy tale, but the Magic Carpet is a beginner's best friend at ski resorts. The Magic Carpet is a special kind of ski lift, perfect for beginners. Unlike ski lifts with chairs or gondolas that take you up high, the Magic Carpet is a moving walkway that stays close to the ground. It's like an escalator you'd find in a shopping mall but designed to work on the snow and take skiers and snowboarders up gentle slopes.

The Magic Carpet usually serves the beginner area at a ski resort. These areas are often called "bunny slopes" and have shorter, easier slopes that are ideal for practicing basic moves like stopping, turning, and getting comfortable on skis. Since the Magic Carpet is slow, steady, and close to the ground, it's a fantastic place to start.

## How to Use the Magic Carpet

Using the Magic Carpet is easy, but there are a few tips to keep in mind for a smooth experience:

1. **Stand Steady**

   When it's your turn, carefully step onto the moving carpet with both skis. Keep your skis straight and close together, pointing uphill. Try not to move too much or lift your skis—just let the carpet do the work.

2. **Look Forward**

   As you ride the Magic Carpet, keep looking forward, not down at your skis. It's best to stay relaxed, with your knees slightly bent for balance. This will make it easier for you to keep your balance and will help you feel comfortable as the carpet moves you up the hill.

3. **Stay in Control**

   Avoid turning your skis or shifting your weight too much while on the Magic Carpet. If your skis start to turn sideways, it can be hard to keep your balance. Just relax and let the carpet take you up.

4. **Getting Off the Carpet**

   When you reach the top, you'll see a small platform or exit area. Here, simply step off the Magic Carpet and glide forward. Try to leave the exit area quickly so others behind you can step off safely too.

After riding the Magic Carpet to the top, you're in the perfect spot to practice your skiing. The gentle slope in the beginner area is ideal for trying out your first moves.

## The Ski Lift/ Ski Lines

Once you've gotten comfortable on the beginner slopes and used the Magic Carpet, you might feel ready to explore other parts of the mountain. That's where the ski lift comes in! The ski lift is your ticket to bigger runs, scenic views, and more adventures. A ski lift is a transportation system that carries skiers and snowboarders from the bottom to higher areas on the mountain. There are different types of ski lifts, but the most common one you'll see is a **chairlift**. Chairlifts have seats that hang from a moving cable, and they scoop up riders, carrying them up the mountain.

Another type you may see is a **gondola**—an enclosed lift that looks like a small cabin. Gondolas protect you from the wind and snow, making them a great option on colder days.

### Ski Lines: Getting Ready for the Lift

Before you even get on the ski lift, there's an important step: getting in line. Here's how to navigate the ski line smoothly.

**1. Know Where to Go**

Most ski resorts have signs and markers to guide you to the correct lift lines. Some lines are dedicated for beginners or go to specific areas of the mountain. Look for signs indicating where the line starts and follow the crowd to get to the right place.

## 2. Wait Your Turn

When you arrive at the line, wait patiently for your turn. As you get closer to the lift entrance, staff members might direct you to a specific lane or group you with other skiers. You'll often join up with other skiers to fill each chair. Don't worry if you end up with people you don't know; it's common to share lifts with other skiers.

## 3. Stay with Your Group

If you're skiing with friends or family, stick together in line to make sure you all get on the same chair. Some resorts have signs indicating how many people each lift can hold—typically two, four, or six riders. Knowing this will help you organize your group before reaching the front of the line.

## Getting on the Ski Lift

Riding the lift is pretty straightforward once you know what to expect. Here's a step-by-step guide for a smooth experience:

### 1. Approach the Loading Zone

As you get to the front of the line, you'll see a marked area called the **loading zone**. This is where you wait for the chairlift to swing around and pick you up. Staff might remind you to watch for the next chair and be ready to sit down.

### 2. Line Up with the Chair

When it's your turn, line up with your group and look behind you to see the chair approaching. Keep your skis pointed straight ahead and be ready to slide forward a little when the chair gets close.

### 3. Sit Down Smoothly

When the chair arrives, gently sit back as it scoops you up. You don't need to jump or hop; just let it catch you, and sit down.

### 4. Pull Down the Safety Bar

Most chairlifts have a safety bar that you can pull down once you're seated. This bar provides extra security as you go up the mountain. Hold onto it lightly and enjoy the ride!

**Tip!** If the chair is moving to fast you can always ask the attendant by the chair to slow it down as you sit!

### Enjoying the Ride

The ski lift ride is a great time to rest your legs, enjoy the view, plan your next run, or even play a game. Here are some things to keep in mind while you're on the lift:

1. **Stay Seated and Steady**
   Keep your back against the seat and your skis pointed forward. Avoid moving around too much, as this can make the lift feel less stable.
2. **Don't Drop Anything!**
   If you're holding ski poles, keep them on your lap or in one hand. Be careful with phones, gloves, or other items, as it can

be tricky to retrieve anything that falls while you're on the lift.

3. **Chat, Plan, Play a Game!**
If you're with friends or family, this is a great time to talk about which trails you want to try next, discuss where to meet, or just play a game!

## Unloading at the Top

When you're near the top of the lift, you'll see signs indicating that it's time to get ready to unload. Here's what to do:

**1. Raise the Safety Bar**

About 50-100 feet before the unloading zone, lift the safety bar and get ready to stand up.

**2. Point Your Skis Forward**

When the chair reaches the unloading zone, gently stand up and slide off the seat, keeping your skis pointed straight ahead. The momentum of the lift and a downward slop will help you glide away from the chair.

**3. Clear the Area Quickly**

Once you're off the lift, move out of the unloading zone quickly to make space for the next group. Find a spot to stop and regroup if you need to, especially if you're skiing with others.

## Chair Lift Games

Once you're comfortable riding the chairlift, it can become one of the most enjoyable parts of your ski day! It's a chance to relax, enjoy the view, and even play a few games to pass the time. Chairlift games are a fun way to connect with friends, and build excitement for your next run. In this chapter, we'll cover some favorite chairlift games that are easy, fun, and perfect for all ages.

### 1. I Spy
**How to Play:**
"I Spy" is a classic game that works perfectly on a chairlift. One person picks something they see,

gives a hint, and the other riders have to guess what it is.

**Example:**

"I spy with my little eye, something that is... green!" The others might guess trees, someone's ski jacket, or a distant sign.

**Tips:**

Try picking objects on the mountain, people skiing below, or something on a distant peak. It's a great way to engage with the landscape around you and practice observation skills!

**2. The Story Game**

**How to Play:**

This is a collaborative storytelling game where each person adds a sentence to create a silly story. The first player begins with a sentence, and each player adds to it in turn.

**Example Start:**

"One day, a skiing penguin decided to try the tallest mountain..."

**Tips:**

The story can be as wild as you like! This game is a great way to spark creativity and have some laughs on the way up the mountain. See if you can finish the story by the time you reach the top.

### 3. 20 Questions (Ski Version)

**How to Play:**

In this game, one person thinks of something related to skiing or the mountain, like "goggles" or "snowboard," and the others have 20 questions to figure out what it is. The questions have to be "yes" or "no" questions.

**Example Questions:**
- "Is it something you wear?"
- "Can you see it from the lift?"
- "Is it made of metal?"

**Tips:**

This game can be as easy or as challenging as you like. If everyone is new to skiing, keep it simple by picking common ski gear or mountain sights.

### 4. Categories Game

**How to Play:**

In this game, one player picks a category, and everyone takes turns naming something that fits in that category. If someone repeats an answer or takes too long to think of something, they're out! You keep playing until only one player remains.

**Example Categories:**
- Ski gear (like goggles, helmet)
- Snacks (Like cookies, potato chips)
- Plants (like pine tree, sun flower)
- Cereals (like frosted flakes)
- Colors ( like red, magenta, blue)

# Mountain Safety

Skiing is an incredible adventure, and part of enjoying it fully is understanding how to stay safe on the mountain. Being aware of your surroundings, following certain rules, and knowing how to handle different situations will help you have fun while staying safe. In this chapter, we'll cover the basics of mountain safety, from skiing smart to what to do if you get separated from your group.

## 1. Know the Ski Run Rating System

One of the first things to understand about mountain safety is the ski run rating system, which tells you the difficulty level of each slope. Here's a quick refresher on common trail markings:

- **Green Circle**: Beginner-friendly slopes that are gentler and less steep.
- **Blue Square**: Intermediate trails with steeper slopes and more turns.
- **Black Diamond**: Advanced trails that are steep and challenging.

It's important to choose runs that match your skill level to avoid getting into trouble. Start with green runs until you feel comfortable, and only move to blue or black runs when you're ready.

## 2. Follow the Skier's Code

Most ski resorts have rules known as the Skier's Responsibility Code, which helps keep everyone on the mountain safe. Here are some key points:

- **Look Uphill Before Starting**: Always check for other skiers above you before merging onto a run.
- **Stay in Control**: Keep your speed at a level you can handle, and be ready to stop or turn when needed.
- **Give Space to Others**: Don't cut off other skiers or make wide turns in crowded areas. Overall give others plenty of space.
- **Yield to People Below You**: When you're skiing down, the people in front of you have the right of way.
- **Obey Signs and Markings**: If you see a sign indicating a closed trail, avoid it. These are closed for a reason, like difficult conditions or avalanche danger.

Remembering these basic rules makes skiing safer and more enjoyable for everyone!

### 3. Be Aware of Hazards

Every mountain has natural features that can be both beautiful and hazardous. Here's what to watch out for:

- **Trees and Rocks**: Stay in the center of the trail and avoid skiing too close to trees, rocks, and other obstacles. Tree wells, which are holes formed around tree trunks in deep snow, can be particularly dangerous.
- **Icy Spots**: Some parts of the trail might be icy, especially in shaded areas. Keep an eye out for shiny, hard-packed sections, and slow down if you see them.
- **Weather Changes**: Conditions on the mountain can change quickly, bringing snowstorms, fog, or strong winds. If visibility drops, ski more slowly and stay with your group.

**4. Take Breaks and Stay Hydrated**

Mountain activities can be exhausting, especially at higher altitudes where the air is thinner. To keep your energy up and stay safe:

- **Take Frequent Breaks**: Skiing requires a lot of focus and energy, so be sure to take breaks throughout the day.

Resting helps you stay alert, which keeps you safer.

- **Drink Water**: Staying hydrated is crucial on the mountain, even if you don't feel thirsty. Pack a small water bottle or plan breaks at the lodge to drink water regularly.
- **Listen to Your Body**: If you're feeling too tired, cold, or even dizzy, it's okay to stop for the day or take a long break. Pushing through when you're tired increases the risk of accidents.

**5. Skiing with a Buddy or Group**

Skiing with friends or family members isn't just more fun—it's also safer! Here's how to make the most of group skiing:

- **Stick Together**: Plan to meet at specific spots, like the end of a run or at the lift line. Skiing close to each other makes it easier to help each other if someone falls or gets lost.
- **Set a Meeting Point**: In case you get separated, agree on a meeting spot like

the lodge or a certain lift. This way, everyone knows where to regroup.
- **Keep an Eye Out for Each Other**: If you're skiing with kids or beginners, make sure to check on them frequently. Offer help or encouragement, and make sure everyone is comfortable.

**6. What to Do if You Fall**

Falling is a normal part of skiing, and sometimes you'll need to get yourself up, brush off the snow, and keep going. Here's a quick guide for safe recovery after a fall:
- **Stay Calm**: Take a moment to assess your surroundings and make sure you're not in the path of other skiers.
- **Get Back Up Safely**: To get up, roll onto your side, then push yourself up to a sitting position. From there, dig your skis into the snow and stand up.
- **Signal for Help if Needed**: If you're injured or in a spot where you can't get up, wave your ski poles above your head to signal for help. Save ski patrols phone

number to your phone for quick dialing in case of emergencys.

**7. Dealing with Getting Lost**

Getting separated from your group or off-track can be a little scary, but if you know what to do, it's no big deal:

- **Stay Calm and Look for Landmarks**: Stop and take a look around. Sometimes you'll spot familiar landmarks, like a trail sign or a chairlift, that can help you get back on track.
- **Ask for Help**: If you're near other skiers or ski patrol staff, ask them for directions. Ski patrollers are there to help you stay safe, and they'll know how to guide you back.
- **Stay Put if You're Unsure**: If you're really unsure of where you are and it's not safe to keep going, find a visible spot and wait. Ski patrol will help you if you're in a tricky spot.

**8. Know When to Call It a Day**

It's tempting to squeeze in "just one more run," but sometimes it's better to call it a day for safety reasons. Here are signs it might be time to head back:

- **Weather is Worsening**: If it's getting windy, foggy, or dark, skiing becomes more dangerous. Better to finish on a high note!

- **Feeling Exhausted or Sore**: Accidents are more likely when you're tired. If your legs are sore or you're feeling worn out, take a break or finish up for the day.

- **Gear or Equipment Problems**: If your gear is feeling uncomfortable or something is loose or broken, stop and have it checked. Proper gear is essential to staying safe.

Mountain safety is all about staying alert, using common sense, and respecting the people and natural beauty around you. When you follow the basics of mountain safety, you set yourself up for a fun, secure experience on the slopes.

Remember, skiing isn't just about speed and excitement—it's also about taking in the view, breathing in the fresh mountain air, and enjoying each moment of the journey. With these tips, you'll be ready to make the most of every ski day safely.

# Ski School - What to Expect

If you're new to skiing or want to improve your skills, ski school is a fantastic place to start. With friendly instructors, fun activities, and special games, ski school makes learning to ski exciting and safe. Whether it's your first day or you're coming back for more lessons, this chapter will give you an idea of what to expect at ski school, from meeting your instructor to trying out cool new skills on the slopes!

**1. Getting Started: Meet Your Instructor and Group**

On your first day, you'll check in at the ski school area and be introduced to your instructor and the other kids in your group. Here's what typically happens:

- **Meet Your Instructor**: Your instructor is there to guide you, teach you skills, and make sure you're comfortable. They'll introduce themselves and tell you about the day's plan.
- **Get to Know Your Group**: You'll be grouped with other kids who are around your age and skill level. Skiing with kids who are learning the same things is fun and helps you make new friends on the mountain.
- **Warm-Up**: You might start with some stretches or easy moves to get ready. Warming up helps loosen your muscles and get you excited to start skiing.

## 2. Learning the Basics (or Getting a Refresher)

Ski school is designed to teach new skills step by step. If you're brand new to skiing, your instructor will start with the basics, like we reviewed in earlier chapters. If you've skied before, your instructor might give you a quick refresher on these basics before moving on to new skills. They'll make sure everyone is comfortable and ready before heading to the slopes.

## 3. Practicing Skills with Games and Activities

Ski school isn't just about drills; instructors make it fun by teaching skills through games and activities. Here are a few common ones:

- **Follow the Leader**: The instructor leads, and everyone follows, practicing turns, stops, or other skills.
- **Obstacle Courses**: Sometimes there's an obstacle course set up with small bumps, cones, or tunnels to ski around. It's a great way to practice control and balance.

- **Ski Races**: For a bit of friendly competition, you might have short, easy races. It's all about learning to control your speed and direction while having fun.

Each activity helps you develop balance, control, and confidence on your skis, making learning feel like play.

## 4. Heading to the Beginner Slopes

Once everyone is ready, it's time to head to the beginner slopes. At most ski schools, these are gentle slopes designed for new skiers. Your instructor will be nearby the entire time to give tips, encouragement, and reminders on how to stay balanced and have fun.

## 7. Taking Breaks and Enjoying the Lodge

Learning to ski takes energy, so your group will take breaks to rest and re-energize. During a break, you might:

- **Go to the Lodge**: Many ski schools have scheduled breaks at the lodge or

designated ski school areas where you can warm up, enjoy a snack, and chat with your group.
- **Enjoy a Hot Chocolate**: A warm drink like hot chocolate can be the perfect way to recharge.
- **Reflect on What You've Learned**: Breaks are also a great time to ask your instructor questions or talk about your favorite parts of the lesson so far.

Remember, it's okay to need breaks—it helps you keep up your energy and stay focused.

**8. Ski School Tips**

It's normal to feel nervous when learning something new, especially a fast-paced sport like skiing. ski school, instructors are there to support you and help you, take advantage of time you have you're your instructors, ask any questions you have, and have them help you set skiing goals

# Après-Ski – Relaxing After a Day on the Slopes

After an exciting day on the slopes, your body is ready for a break, and it's time to relax, refuel, and enjoy some fun activities off the mountain. Après-ski (French for "after skiing") is all about unwinding, spending time with family and friends, and getting ready for the next day's adventure. Here's how to make the most of your time after skiing, from taking care of sore muscles to cozy activities that bring a perfect end to a ski day!

Before we unwind, its important to make sure you take care of your ski gear. Proper care helps your equipment last longer, keeps it performing well, and ensures you're ready for your next day on the mountain.

## 1. Drying and Storing Your Gear

Skiing can make everything damp, from your clothes to your boots and gloves. Drying everything out is the first step to keeping your gear in top shape.

- **Ski Boots**: Take your boots off and buckle them back to the size you wear them at, this helps ski boots keep their shape and makes them last longer and be more comfortable. After, set them somewhere warm and dry, like near a heater or in a cozy room. Drying out the boots helps prevent any musty smells and keeps your boots comfortable for the next day.
- **Gloves and Mittens**: Wet gloves are no fun the next day! Hang them up somewhere warm and spread the fingers apart to let air flow inside. Make sure they're completely dry before putting them away.
- **Jacket and Pants**: Snow can sometimes sneak into your clothing. Hang up your jacket and pants to air dry

in a warm spot, even if they don't feel too wet. This prevents any moisture from getting trapped inside, which can make them chilly for your next outing.

- **Goggles**: Take your Goggles off your helmet and store them in a protective pouch, this will ensure the strap doesn't get overly stretched from the helmet and prevent scratches on the lens. Store in a warm dry room.
- **Skis and Poles**: Store in a dry place where they can drip dry until the next time you go skiing
- **Wash Your Base Layers and Socks**: Wearing fresh, clean layers each day helps you stay warm and comfortable. Wash your base layers, socks, and any neck warmers after each day on the slopes.
- **Keep Track of Accessories**: Neck warmers, hats, and gloves are easy to lose track of, especially after a full day of skiing. Make a habit of organizing them

in a specific spot, like a gear bag or a basket at home, so you know where everything is next time.

Caring for your ski gear doesn't just keep it looking nice; it helps it perform better and last longer. When your skis are free of rust, your boots are dry, and your clothes are clean, you're more comfortable and prepared to hit the slopes. Plus, it makes skiing feel even more fun and exciting when you know your gear is ready to go. Now we are finally ready for Après-ski

## Après-ski

### 1. Warming Up and Getting Cozy

Once you're done skiing, the first thing you'll want to do is warm up and change out of your ski clothes. Here's how to get comfortable and cozy after being out in the snow:

- **Change Into Comfy Clothes**: Swap your ski clothes for warm, dry clothes.

Fuzzy socks, soft sweaters, and comfy pants are perfect for après-ski.
- **Enjoy a Hot Drink**: Warming up with a hot chocolate, tea, or warm apple cider can be a delicious way to shake off the chill from a day outside.
- **Cozy Up by the Fire**: If there's a fireplace where you're staying, find a cozy spot by it. Reading a book, talking with friends, or just watching the fire can be super relaxing after skiing.

Getting comfortable after a day on the mountain helps your body relax and recharges your energy.

## 2. Stretching and Relaxing Your Muscles

Skiing uses a lot of different muscles, so stretching can help prevent soreness and make sure you're ready for your next day on the slopes.
- **Gentle Stretching**: Focus on stretching your legs, back, and arms.

Gentle stretches help ease any stiffness and keep your muscles flexible.
- **Foam Rolling**: If you have a foam roller, use it to massage your legs, especially your thighs and calves. This can help relax tight muscles.
- **Take a Warm Bath**: If you're feeling especially sore, a warm bath can feel amazing after skiing. Add some bubbles or bath salts for extra relaxation.

Stretching and relaxing your muscles after skiing helps your body recover faster and makes it easier to get back out on the slopes the next day.

### 3. Refueling with Good Food

After a big day of skiing, your body needs some good food to refuel. Here are some popular après-ski foods and snacks to help you regain your energy:

- **Warm Soups and Stews**: Hot soups like chicken noodle, tomato, or vegetable

stew are comforting and filling. They also help warm you up from the inside.
- **Hearty Snacks**: Cheese and crackers, pretzels, or a bowl of popcorn are great for a quick snack before dinner. You'll probably be hungrier than usual, so healthy snacks can help keep you going.
- **Dinner Time**: Many people love to gather for a big dinner after skiing. This might be a pizza night, pasta, or a cozy meal at a mountain restaurant with family and friends.

Eating good food helps your body recover, so you feel strong and ready for another day on the slopes.

### 4. Après-Ski Games and Activities

Après-ski is about more than just relaxing; it's also a time to have fun with friends and family. Here are some activities that can make the evening enjoyable:

- **Board Games**: Classics like Uno, Monopoly, or Scrabble are fun to play as a group. Playing games gives everyone a chance to laugh and unwind together.

- **Movie or Show Night**: After dinner, snuggle up and watch a fun family movie or TV show. Ski movies or winter-themed cartoons can be extra fun when you're on a ski trip.
- **Story Time**: Sharing stories from the day—like funny moments on the slopes, impressive runs, or silly falls—is a great way to bond with friends and family. You can take turns telling stories, or even make up funny skiing adventures.

These activities make après-ski feel special and help create lasting memories with the people you're skiing with.

### 5. Reflecting on Your Skiing Progress

Each day you ski, you're building your skills and growing as a skier. Taking a few moments to reflect on your progress is a great way to end the day.

- **Think About Your Favorite Part of the Day**: Was there a particular run you enjoyed or a skill you felt proud of? Celebrating small victories can help you recognize how much you're improving.
- **Set Goals for Tomorrow**: Whether it's practicing turns, trying a new run, or just having fun, think about what you'd like to work on next time. Having goals makes skiing even more exciting.
- **Write in a Ski Journal**: If you're keeping a journal, jot down a few notes about your day. Writing about your favorite parts and things you'd like to work on can help you remember your ski trip.

Reflecting on your day and setting goals helps you feel more confident and focused for the next day on the mountain.

# Embrace Your Skiing Adventure

Congratulations! You've reached the end of *The Skiing Handbook*. By now, you've learned so much about skiing—from what it is and how to prepare, to taking care of your gear and enjoying the après-ski life. Skiing is an exciting adventure filled with fun, challenges, and unforgettable moments, and you're now equipped with the knowledge to make the most of your time on the slopes.

### Celebrate Your Progress

Remember, every skier starts somewhere. It's perfectly normal to feel nervous or unsure, especially on your first few days out. The most important thing is to keep trying and have fun! Celebrate the small victories—whether it's mastering the pizza technique, feeling confident on the magic carpet, or taking your first ride on a ski lift. Each time you hit the slopes, you're learning, growing, and becoming a better skier.

## Skiing is More Than Just a Sport

Skiing isn't just about racing down a mountain; it's also about enjoying the beautiful winter scenery, spending time with family and friends, and creating lasting memories. The laughter, the hot chocolate breaks, and the fun games you play after a long day all add to the joy of skiing. Embrace the entire experience—the thrill of the slopes and the warmth of après-ski!

## Keep Exploring and Learning

As you continue your skiing journey, don't forget to explore new places, try different runs, and even consider taking lessons to improve your skills. Skiing is a sport that can be enjoyed for a lifetime, and there's always something new to learn. Whether you're a beginner or an experienced skier, keep pushing your limits and trying new things.

## Join the Ski Community

Skiing is also about community. Don't hesitate to make friends on the slopes or join ski clubs.

The ski community is filled with supportive people who share your passion for winter sports. Sharing tips, experiences, and laughs with others makes skiing even more enjoyable.

**Your Next Adventure Awaits!**

So, as you put away this book and gear up for your next adventure, remember: each day on the mountain is a new opportunity to learn, have fun, and enjoy the magic of skiing. Whether you're gliding down a snowy slope, taking a moment to appreciate the breathtaking views, or sharing a laugh with friends, embrace every moment.

Thank you for joining me on this journey through the world of skiing. Now, it's time to get out there and make your skiing dreams come true. Have fun, stay safe, and enjoy every second on the slopes. Happy skiing!

Printed in Great Britain
by Amazon